More praise for Luigi Fontanella's Bertgang.

In *Bertgang* "soul" is apparition, "imago eterna," cast however in the flow of the mysterious events and motivations that lead one to the urgency of a summarizing form. This "imago eterna," the soul that shows itself, has the nature of the being that it already is. It is, for example, [Leopardi's] Silvia invented at the window, in her being eternal and at the same time severed youth, contemplated in the fullness of the rose and in the fading of the asphodel. In this work — consistent with his entire poetic journey — Fontanella senses the precariousness of the condition of the word; his is a stubbornly and firmly analogical poetry, at the expense of a very widespread semantic "I couldn't care less attitude," that knows how to bet on the power of the symbol as a living entity among us, "immagine rimossa, ma in / grado di ritornare per puro / di dottrina! Quella / che ci tiene lontani dalla vita... / Dunque fedele nell'infedeltà / perché dimenticare non vuol dire eliminare / ciò a cui si era legati." Here it is: this Gradiva Bertgang, advancing with the cadenced and sure step of the god Mars toward a frontal reality, speaks to us of a time that does not belong to us, that has never belonged to us, and looking at us invites us to contemplate the imago of the eternal becoming time in us, telling us that we can resist time only in the moment of an ephemeral splendor.

—Sebastiano Aglieco

Luigi Fontanella's *Bertgang* appears to be a brief guide to advancing within the framework of a broad signification of the Italian poetic landscape of which Fontanella is an important component. Inspired by Wilhelm Jensen's story "Gradiva–Fantasia Pompeiana," we witness Luigi's current fusion to retrace, alongside the eyes of his Zoe-Bertgang-Gradiva-Irene, the grid of a dreamed existence, its acerbic accurate meaning through the junctions of this poem characterized by the sound of particular grace.

— Aldo Gerbino

Bertgang is a complex, multifaceted book. As in some of Fontanella's seminal works, both in verse and prose, it is time that plays with men. But the author has too vivid and pronounced a sense of life, of carnality, of the tenacity of the search for meaning and sensuality, to simply give his works a uniquely elegiac flavor, an unconditional surrender to transience. It is probably no coincidence that, as was the case with the protagonist of his novel *Controfigura* (Marsilio, 2009), the action that spontaneously, naturally accompanies the act of thinking, reflecting and dreaming, is motion, stepping, exploring the world, inner and outer, through walking. The name of the protagonist of this poem, Gradiva, means "she who advances." That is, she who physically proceeds, not only on a dream level, from one place to another, from one dimension to the adjacent one, from one moment to the next. (...) A book that is not easy to read, therefore, that demands attention and invites one to broaden one's spaces and horizons, penetrating, meter by meter, the steep and friable terrain of the senses, both physical and psychological.

— Ivano Mugnaini

As vibrantly inspired and dreamlike as the very subject matter of the tale, Luigi Fontanella's *Bertgang* seems to be one of those works that have been waiting for a poet forever, and whose realization seems only to depend on the happiness of an encounter, a reading, a life experience. Now that it is there, it seems to retroactively illuminate a whole poetic and narrative path, and make it shine — as if magically — with a new light.

— Giancarlo Pontiggia

Bertgang
Fantasia onirica

An Oneiric Phantasy

LUIGI FONTANELLA

Translated and with an introductory note by
Michael Palma

CASA LAGO PRESS
NEW FAIRFIELD, CT

Diaspora
Volume 6

As "diaspora" is the dispersion or spread of people from their original homeland, this book series takes its name in the intellectual spirit of willful dispersion of subject matter and thought. It is dedicated to publishing those studies and creative works that in various and sundry ways either speak to or offer new methods of analysis and/or articulations of the Italian diaspora.

The publication of this book has bene made possible through a generous grant from an anonymous donor who wishes not to be identified but urges others to donate to historical and cultural studies.

Cover art by Francesca R. Pasqualini

ISBN 978-1-955995-11-5
Library of Congress Control Number: Available upon request

© 2025 Michael Palma, "Translation"
© 2025 Luigi Fontanella

All rights reserved.
Printed in the United States of America

CASA LAGO PRESS
New Fairfield, CT

*a Irene, che un giorno vidi passare in una strada
di St. Louis*

*to Irene, whom I saw passing by one day on a street
in St. Louis*
L. F.

*For Donna and Ernest Montenegro, my first friends
in a new land*
M. P.

TABLE OF CONTENTS

Translator's Note, by Michael Palma (vii)

BERTGANG (12)

Author's Note (65)

About the Author and Translator (75)

Translator's Note

It is as fashionable nowadays to disparage Sigmund Freud as it was previously to praise him. Despite the many attacks, some of which have merit, on his theories and the extent of his influence, I still find his analysis of the human personality, its motives, and its behaviors more persuasive and satisfying than any alternative explanation. When I first became acquainted with my wife, an enthusiasm for Freud's views was one of the many things we found we had in common. Nonetheless, I somehow managed to get through a good deal of my adult life without ever having heard of Freud's commentary on Wilhelm Jensen's *Gradiva*, or of *Gradiva* itself, or of Jensen, for that matter — gaps in my education that were not filled in until I asked Luigi Fontanella how the journal that he has directed for more than forty years got its name.

Having introduced me to these works many years ago, he subsequently deepened my pleasure in them — and that of many other readers — with his own response to them in the form of his narrative poem *Bertgang*. In writing a literary work of his own inspired by a beloved text, he contributes to a tradition that extends at least as far back as Virgil's *Aeneid* and as far forward as Derek Walcott's *Omeros*. The transposition from prose to verse is not Fontanella's only significant innovation. Jensen's novella is narrated in the third person, with its central figure, Norbert Hanold, observed from the outside. By directly assuming the consciousness and the voice of the protagonist (as did Guido Gozzano in his recasting of Bernardin de Saint-Pierre's *Paul et Virginie*), Fontanella adds freshness and immediacy to the old tale, placing us inside the confusion, the frustration, and ultimately the delight of the character's situation.

In his Author's Note, which appears at the end of this volume, he describes *Bertgang* as "[a]n experiment that is also or principally linguistic (to reproduce in poetry, with an appropriate rhythm, the magical and *distant* aura in which the event unfolds that is narrated by Jensen and so acutely retraced by Freud)." In seeking to reproduce his work as faithfully as possible, I have followed him in his frequent use of pentameter and of diction lightly flavored with the poetic styles of past times, bringing, I hope, the same enthusiasm and care to re-creating his work that he brought to re-imagining that of Jensen.

M. P.

Siamo di un giorno.
Uno, che è?
Nessuno, che è?
Sogno di un'ombra è l'uomo.
— Pindaro

Caccia pure la natura con la forca,
continuerà a ritornare.
— Orazio

Nuovo pensiero dentro a me si mise,
Del qual più altri nacquero e diversi;
E tanto d'uno in altro vaneggiai,
Che gli occhi per vaghezza ricopersi,
E il pensamento in sogno trasmutai.
— Dante, *Purgatorio*, XVIII, 141-145

> We are creatures of a day.
> What are we?
> What are we not?
> Man is the dream of a shadow.
> —Pindar

> Though you drive away nature with a pitchfork,
> it will keep on coming back.
> —Horace

> I felt a new thought form itself in me
> and that thought led to many various
>   thoughts with which my mind began to teem,
>   and rambling there I closed my eyes, and thus
> my musings were transmuted to a dream.
> —Dante, *Purgatorio*, XVIII, 141-145

Bertgang
Fantasia onirica

Bertgang
An Oneiric Phantasy

I

Nella breve ora degli spiriti
una giovane ragazza uscì di casa
e si diresse con passo rapido e leggero
verso la dimora di Meleagro. Qui giunta
scomparve come d'incanto
fra le colonne della corte.
Una graziosa farfalla
aveva svolazzato un attimo prima attorno a lei,
farfalla dell'Ade messaggera
che l'invitava a rientrare
essendo già trascorsa la sua breve ora...
Trasognato le gridai: "Tornerai
ancora qui domani all'ora meridiana? Dimmi
se corporea sei o puro spirito vagante." Ebbro
e trepidante, così le domandavo
mentre lei già spariva.

I

In the evanescent hour of the spirits
there was a girl who came out of her house
to make her way with light and rapid steps
toward the abode of Meleager. Arriving there
she vanished as if enchanted
between the courtyard's columns.
A graceful butterfly
had been fluttering all about her a moment before,
Hades' messenger butterfly
bidding her to return
because her fleeting hour had already passed...
I called to her dreamily: "Will you come back
to this same spot at noon tomorrow? Tell me,
are you corporeal or a pure wandering spirit?" Anxious
and enraptured, I questioned her, who meanwhile
had already disappeared.

*Tanta era la strada che avevo fatta
dalla mia città a quella contrada
da me tanto amata per pura
passione di dottrina. Annoiato
e saturo dopo lunghe ore
piegato sui miei libri
una mattina udii fuori dalla finestra
il cinguettio d'un canarino
rinchiuso in una gabbia
(come lo ero io fra carte e documenti)
che solo con il proprio canto
lanciava al mondo l'innato
impulso a fuggirsene dalla sua prigione.
Quel cinguettio mi portò alla finestra
e di sotto per la strada
la vidi improvvisamente passare… era lei
la mia tanto studiata Gradiva – questo
il nome che le avevo dato in onore
di Marte Gradivo, come gli antichi poeti
chiamavano questo dio avanzante
verso il combattimento… – Sì, era lei,
che ora con passo rapido e leggero
attraversava la strada. Mi precipitai
per le scale ma giunto sulla via
non riuscii, data la ressa, più a trovarla.
Dovevo partire
per andarla a studiare più da vicino
là dove uno scultore l'aveva ritratta
per le antiche vie di Pompei
con quel suo passo… il piede
destro in posizione quasi verticale, mentre
con la mano sinistra teneva
un po' sollevato l'orlo della gonna…
un modo di procedere che solo
a una giovane donna può appartenere.*

*So long was the road that I had made
from my city to that open place
out in the countryside that I loved so
out of pure zeal for learning. Sated
and saturated after long hours
bending over my books
one morning I could hear outside my window
the chirping and twittering of a canary
closed up in a cage
(just as I was amid documents and papers)
who all alone with his own song
hurled to the world his innate
impulse to fly away from his prison cell.
That chirping drew me over to the window
and down below I suddenly
saw her pass by along the road... it was
Gradiva whom I'd read so much about —
this was the name I'd given her in honor
of Mars Gradivus, as the ancient poets
had called this mighty god advancing toward
the field of battle... Truly, it was she,
who with her rapid and lightfooted steps
was moving along the road. I hurried down
the stairs, but when I came out on the street,
amid the crowd, I couldn't find her there.
I needed to set out,
go where I could examine much more closely
how a sculptor had portrayed her moving
through the ancient Pompeian streets
with that same step... her right
foot raised and virtually vertical, while with
her left hand she held the hem
of her flowing gown a bit above the ground...
a way of carrying herself that could
belong to no one else than a young woman.*

Il giorno dopo l'attesi ansioso
davanti alla casa di Meleagro.
Poco prima di arrivarvi
colsi un fresco ramo d'asfodelo
pensando quanto inutile
fosse tutto il mio sapere
e quanto indifferente il mondo ad esso.
Ansioso ero e malinconico perché
temevo non le fosse permesso
un altro ritorno
se non molto tempo dopo...
tanto ansioso
che quando lei riapparve
pensai fosse soltanto un'illusione
tra me e me mormoravo: "Tu non ci sei
veramente, tu non vivi ancora!"

The following day I waited anxiously
for her outside the house of Meleager.
Shortly before arriving there
I'd gathered a fresh sprig of asphodel
thinking about the uselessness
of all my erudition
and of the world's indifference to it.
I was anxious, I was melancholy
because I feared she wouldn't be allowed
to reappear again
until much later on...
so anxious
that when she reappeared
I thought that it was only an illusion
before me, and I muttered to myself:
"You aren't really here, you're not alive!"

Lei invece d'improvviso ricomparve
sulla via di Mercurio
di luce dorata avvolta... io intravidi
subito il suo profilo, il suo passo
agile e leggero, pura
immagine di sogno ma reale.
Sull'ultima pietra del suo passaggio
se ne stava immobile
distesa sotto il rovente sole
una grande lucertola, che m'inviava
fino agli occhi
riflessi d'oro e malachite.
Ma al sopraggiungere del piede di Gradiva
essa sguciò via rapidamente
sul nero rilucente lastricato. Sorridente
mi rivolse la parola
chiedendomi se le avevo portato
il bianco fiore dell'oblio. Io le guardai
i piedi che non portavano sandali
come avevo immaginato
ma scarpe chiare color sabbia. Sorpresa
e ironica diceva: "Non chiamarmi
Gradiva, il mio nome è Zoe,
non spirito sono, ma vita. La tua
malinconia si conviene a una morta
che solo per brevi ore torna in vita."
Lucidi i bei capelli bruni
la fronte alabastrina, due occhi
fissi e scintillanti su di me.
"Sei tu Atalanta, la figlia di Iafo?
O discendi dalla famiglia del poeta Meleagro?"

And yet in fact she'd suddenly appeared
upon the Street of Mercury
wrapped in a golden light... I had a sudden
glimpse of her outline there, of her lightfooted
and nimble step, a pure
image out of a dream but also real.
On the last stone of her passageway
I saw a lizard
stretched motionless out in the scorching sun,
a large lizard lying there and beaming
reflections of gold and malachite
right into my eyes.
But at the approaching footsteps of Gradiva
the lizard scampered rapidly away
over the glittering black pavement. Smiling
she began to speak to me
asking me if I'd brought the white flower
of forgetfulness for her. I looked at her
and saw that on her feet were not the sandals
that I'd imagined there
but bright sand-colored shoes instead. Surprise
and irony in her voice, she said to me:
"Don't call me Gradiva, my name is Zoe,
I'm not a spirit, I'm life. Your melancholy
is better suited to a dead woman who
comes back to life but only for brief moments."
All shining were her beautiful brown hair,
her alabaster brow, her sparkling eyes
focused upon me. "Are you Atalanta,
daughter of Iasus? Or are you descended
from the family of the poet Meleager?"

Muta se ne stava
ma con le labbra come volte a un sorriso…
Una farfalla d'improvviso color rosso e oro
dai papaveri volò sulle colonne,
poi volteggiò sopra il suo capo, infine
si posò sui suoi capelli.
Lei continuava a tacere
e di nuovo, senz'altro dire,
con movimento rapido e tranquillo
scomparve alla mia vista.
La farfalla continuava
a svolazzare sui papaveri
con le sue ali rosso-d'oro porporine.

She said nothing, but
her mouth was turned up as if in a smile...
Then suddenly a red-gold butterfly
flew from the poppies over to the pillars,
fluttered above her head, and finally
settled upon her hair.
Still she didn't speak
and once again, without
another word, with swift untroubled movements
she vanished from my sight.
Still the butterfly
hovered above the poppies,
fluttering its rosy red-gold wings.

Solo restai con me stesso
e di lontano mi trafisse un grido
come uno sghignazzo d'un uccello nero
che volava sopra le rovine. Per terra
era rimasto un quadernetto (un pegno, forse?)
dimenticato da Gradiva. Lo sfogliai
trepidante guardando i disegni a matita
della Pompei antica e di colpo pensai
nulla si dimentica
senza una nascosta ragione.

Left there all alone
I found myself transfixed by a far cry
like the raucous cawing of a blackbird
flying over the ruins. On the ground
there was a little notebook (was it a token?)
Gradiva had forgotten. I leafed through it
with trembling hands, looking at pencil drawings
of ancient Pompeii, struck by the idea
that nothing is forgotten
without some underlying hidden reason.

Continuavo a guardarmi attorno e d'improvviso
scoprii nel muro del porticato
una stretta spaccatura, una fessura
sufficiente a lasciar passare
un'esile creatura come Gradiva.
Era forse questa la via da lei
utilizzata per ritornare alla sua tomba?
E di nuovo sprofondai nel mio
delirio... proprio mentre
una lieve ombra scompariva
in fondo alla Strada dei Sepolcri.
"O fragile Figura, vivi o
immagine sei della mia illusione?"
Ripresi trasognato il mio cammino
mentre in me prendeva forma un impulso
assoluto: se mai l'avessi rivista
le avrei toccato una mano, benché
in me convivesse un sentimento ambiguo:
di dolore se solo aria avessi toccato
di spavento se corporea l'avessi constatata.

Still looking all around, I suddenly
noticed in the wall of the arcade
a narrow cleft, a crack that nonetheless
was wide enough to let a creature through
who was as slender as Gradiva was.
Was this perhaps the passageway that she
made use of in returning to her tomb?
And I was once more sinking into my
delirium... even as
I saw a nimble shadow disappear
at the end of the Avenue of Sepulchers.
"O frail Figure, are you alive or are you
only an image sprung from my illusion?"
Lost in a reverie, I retraced my steps.
Yet all the while an absolute impulse
was taking shape in me: if I should ever
see her again, then I would touch her hand,
in spite of my uncertain expectations:
of pain if I should only touch the air,
of fright if I should prove that she was real.

II

A lungo girovagai immerso
nei pensieri finché i miei passi
mi spinsero per un ignoto sentiero
di fronte a un caseggiato mai
visto prima, presso i ruderi
del grande anfiteatro pompeiano
ove sorgeva un altro domicilio
"L'Albergo del Sole"... Entrai
per rinfrescarmi un poco, vuota
era la sala d'ingresso se non per il fitto
ronzare delle mosche in aria. L'anziano
sfaccendato proprietario mi raccontò di scavi
e di reperti di cui aveva ornato la sua dimora.
"Una giovane coppia di amanti
di fronte alla catastrofe
si era stretta in un ultimo
abbraccio... guardi, questo è un fermaglio
raccolto nella cenere accanto alla ragazza."

II

For a long time I wandered here and there
plunged deep in thought, until my steps
carried me along an unknown path
to stand before a block of houses
I had never seen before, near the ruins of
a large Pompeiian amphitheater
where there stood another building with a sign
that read "The Inn of the Sun"... I went inside
for some refreshment, and found the entranceway
empty but for the thick buzz of the flies
in the air. The elderly proprietor,
with nothing to do, told me of excavations
and the finds with which his place was decorated.
"A couple of young lovers
facing the catastrophe
clasped one another in a last
embrace... look, here's a brooch
gathered from the ashes near the girl."

Volli assolutamente comprare
quel fermaglio, un acquisto
che in altri tempi avrei trovato stolto.
Ma quando uscendo dall'albergo,
intravidi appeso a una finestra
un ramoscello d'asfodelo,
la vista dei suoi bianchi fiori
mi confermò che giusto e legittimo
era stato quel mio strampalato
acquisto. Un pensiero
allora s'impadronì del mio delirio:
e se quella giovane morta
fosse stata la mia Gradiva?
Era forse lei quella ragazza
che uscita per il suo appuntamento
presso la casa di Meleagro
si era poi incontrata con il suo amante amato
e Morte li avesse colti abbracciati?
E quel verde fermaglio
servito a fermarle il vestito al collo
non era forse a lei appartenuto? Ora esso
mi bruciava tra le dita
come fosse di sostanza rovente
procurandomi lo stesso dolore
che immaginavo avrei provato
se poggiando la mia mano sulla sua
soltanto aria avessi incontrato.

I definitely wished to buy
that brooch, a purchase
I would have thought foolish at another time.
But as I was leaving the inn
I caught a glimpse of a small branch
of asphodel at a window,
and the sight of those white flowers
confirmed my sense that this eccentric purchase
had been the right and proper
thing to do. Then a thought
took hold of me in my delirium:
what if that dead young girl
had been my own Gradiva?
Could she be that young woman
who had gone out to keep her assignation
near the house of Meleager
and then met up with the young man she loved
and Death had seized them as they were embracing?
And that green brooch
that had fastened a woman's clothing at her throat,
wasn't it possible it belonged to her?
Now it burned between my fingers
as if it had been red-hot,
arousing in me the same pain
that I imagined would have pierced me there
if I had placed my hand on hers
and encountered only empty air.

Più tardi al "Diomede"
durante la cena due ospiti
nuovi venuti (un lui e una lei:
forse fratelli?) suscitarono la mia
simpatia. Una rosa rossa
sorrentina, sul petto della giovane,
mi risvegliò un certo ricordo
che non riuscii a precisare.
Lieta era la naturalezza affettuosa
di quella coppia, si godeva la vita
senza la minima nube, lontani
da qualsiasi ambascia come la mia
verso una giovinetta morta
venti secoli prima!

Later at the Diomedes
during dinner two newly
arrived guests (a he and a she:
maybe siblings?) caught my
fancy. A red Sorrento
rose on the young woman's breast
stirred in me a certain memory,
one I could not recall in any detail.
That pair possessed a light affectionate
naturalness, they were enjoying life
without the shadow of a cloud, far from
any such feeling as my anguish over
a young girl who had died
twenty centuries ago!

Durante la notte, poi, un incubo
tetro e insensato: in un posto
al sole sedeva Gradiva
un filo d'erba in mano, a mo' di laccio,
intenta a catturare una lucertola... diceva
Sta' fermo... la collega ha ragione
il mezzo è buono, ed è stato
usato con successo...
Riuscii a liberarmi, a difendermi
da questo cupo sogno
con l'aiuto di un invisibile
uccellino, che all'improvviso
lanciò un trillo simile a una risatina
e con il suo stridulo sghignazzo
si portò via la lucertola nel becco.

During the night, much later, a nightmare
crazy and dark: Gradiva was sitting there
in one spot in the sun,
a blade of grass in her hand, in the shape of a noose,
intent on catching a lizard with it... she said
Stay still... my friend is right,
it's a good method, it's been used
successfully before...
I managed to get free, to shield myself
from this abysmal dream
with the aid of an invisible
little bird that had suddenly
let out a trill that sounded like a sneer,
and with its sniggering shrill shriek
it carried off the lizard in its beak.

III

La mattina dopo sotto un cielo
d'azzurro puro un cespuglio
di rose rosse sorrentine
mi spinsero a raccoglierne qualcuna: un gesto
che alleviava la mia mente.
Mi diressi verso Pompei con le rose,
il fermaglio e il quadernetto,
tormentato da mille pensieri e
da una gelosia presente sotto
i più svariati vestimenti. Il sole
quel giorno era impegnato
in una prestazione fuor dell'ordinario
sempre più implacabile... guardavo
le antiche fontane lungo la strada
l'uso continuo che gli assetati di allora
ne avevano fatto per sporgersi
sulla bocchetta di quell'acqua,
ora scomparsa, appoggiavano una mano
sul bordo marmoreo e così
come fanno le gocce che scavano la roccia
questo aveva un po' alla volta
prodotto un'incavatura sul punto
d'appoggio... Anche la mano
di Gradiva s'era forse appoggiata
su quella minuscola incavatura...

III

The following morning under a pure
blue sky a bush of red
Sorrento roses
impelled me to pick a few of them: a gesture
that eased my mind.
I made my way toward Pompeii with the roses,
the brooch and the notebook,
tormented by a thousand thoughts and
by a jealousy coursing under
my varicolored clothes. The sun
was engaged that day
in a performance out of the ordinary,
ever more implacable... I saw
the ancient fountains all along the street
that the parched souls of those times
had put to constant use by leaning
over the little opening
for that now vanished water, resting a hand
on the marble border, and in doing so
as drops of water cut into the rock
they had, an infinitesimal bit at a time,
produced a hollow at the point
of support... And it may be
that even the hand of Gradiva had once been
supported on that tiny hollow there...

Arrivai infine alla Casa del Fauno.
Dietro il peristilio si apriva
un interno magnifico giardino
tutto coperto di papaveri in fiore.
Silenzio e pace ovunque tutt'intorno
ma a un tratto mi fermai stupito:
non ero solo. In un cantuccio intravidi
due figure strettamente abbracciate
tanto da parermi una sola... così
avvinghiati con le braccia, tenevano
le loro bocche strettamente unite
in un sensuale
lungo
appassionato bacio.
Riconobbi in loro la coppia
della sera precedente: due innamorati, certo,
probabili ardenti giovani sposi.
Subito mi ritrassi discreto e inosservato
con un senso di rispetto
che per molto tempo m'era mancato.

Eventually I came to the House of the Faun.
Behind the peristyle there opened up
a truly magnificent interior garden
covered over with poppies in full bloom.
Peace and silence were everywhere about,
but suddenly I stopped in astonishment:
I wasn't alone. Off in a corner I glimpsed
two figures bound in an embrace so tight
they seemed to be a single figure... thus
clutched in one another's arms, they held
their mouths together tightly fused into
a long and
sensual
passionate kiss.
I recognized them as the couple from
the previous evening: two lovers, certainly,
an ardent young married couple, probably.
Quickly, discreetly, unobserved I withdrew
with a feeling of respect
that I had been without for a long time.

Eccomi infine davanti alla Casa
di Meleagro – e se Gradiva fosse
in compagnia? – un panico
timore che m'induce, non appena lei
compare, a chiederle: "Sei sola?"
Di fronte al suo stupore le racconto
tutto il mio ultimo vaneggiamento.
"...Vedo che hai portato l'album
che avevo dimenticato ieri...", poi
guardandomi le mani, "Sembra
che tu sia amico delle rose...
e quel fermaglio l'hai trovato al sole?,
sai, strani scherzi a volte fa quell'astro..."
Così mi parlava sorridente, poi volle
condividere il suo pane. Perfetta
e luminosa era la chiostra dei suoi denti,
ancora sorridendo aggiunse: "Non ti sembra
che già altra volta, duemila anni fa,
mangiammo insieme il nostro pane?"
Scherzava o diceva seriamente?
Tempo era allora che mettessi
in atto il mio esperimento.
La sua mano vidi appoggiata
tranquilla sul ginocchio, una tediosa
mosca vi si era posata – un attimo, e
scattò la mia sulla sua
senza che incontrasse vuota aria.
Secca e sgradita la sua replica: "Tu,
sei pazzo da legare, Norbert!"

I find myself eventually before
the House of Meleager — and if Gradiva
was with someone else? — an irrational
dread that provokes me, as soon as she
appears, to ask her: "Are you alone?"
In the face of her astonishment I recount
all of my latest delirium to her.
"...I see that you are carrying the album
that I'd forgotten yesterday...," and then
looking at my hands, "It seems
that you are fond of roses...
and that brooch, did you find it lying in the sun?
You know, that star can play strange tricks sometimes..."
Smiling she said all this to me, then wished
to share her bread. Perfect and luminous
were her teeth as, still with a smile,
she added: "Don't you feel as if we are
in another time, two thousand years ago,
even as we eat our bread together?"
Was she joking or talking seriously?
I felt then that the time had come for me
to put my experiment into practice.
I saw that her hand was resting peacefully
upon her knee, where a tedious fly
had positioned itself — just one instant, and
my hand took hold of hers
without encountering empty air.
Her response was dry and disagreeable:
"Norbert, you are a raving lunatic!"

Non ebbi tempo di scuotermi
dallo stupore (come sapeva ella
il mio nome?) che già un altro
curioso accadimento
si mostrava ai miei occhi.
Era la coppia della Casa del Fauno,
la giovane diceva: "Anche tu
qui, Zoe? Tu pure in viaggio nuziale?"
Fuggii stordito e vergognoso
e più che mai malato
d'un eccesso di malia.

I hadn't yet had time to shake
my amazement off (how did she know
my name?) when another odd event
had already begun
unfolding before my eyes.
It was the couple from the House of the Faun,
the young woman said: "Are you here too,
Zoe? Are you on your honeymoon like us?"
I fled away, stunned and ashamed
and ill, more ill than I'd ever been before,
from an excess of enchantment.

IV

Mi riportai verso la Strada dei Sepolcri,
occupato a risolvere i residui
elementi del mio dubbio:
davvero folle ero stato a credere Gradiva
quella giovane donna che ora mi parlava
e mi offriva il suo pane? Eppure
non era forse lei, con il suo passo
svelto e lieve, benché per trasposta figura,
la ragazza di cui mi ero innamorato? E la sua
non trasparente mano...
mano calda e materialmente vera?
Vano sogno dunque il mio e solo vera
la mia follia? E come mai
conosceva il mio nome? Meglio
sarebbe stato morir con lei sepolto
duemila anni prima...
Così rimuginavo
guardando la strada a me davanti
ora in tutta la sua malinconica chiarezza,
senza più quel luccichìo
che ricopriva le nere pietre laviche
della strada. Il suo aspetto di morte
era in armonia col proprio nome.

IV

I walked back toward the Street of Sepulchers,
working at resolving the remaining
elements of my uncertainty:
had I been truly mad to think Gradiva
was the young woman who'd talked with me just now
and offered her bread to me? And yet
might she not have really been, with her light and swift
footstep, although she was transposed in form,
the girl with whom I'd fallen in love? And her
untransparent hand...
her hand that was warm and physically real?
Was mine an empty dream and only real
in my madness? And how on earth
did she know my name? It would
be better to have died and been buried with her
two thousand years before...
So I ruminated,
beholding the street before me now
in all its melancholy clarity,
no longer suffused with the glow
that had shimmered over its black lava stones.
Its deathly atmosphere now seemed
to be all of a piece with the name it bore.

Eccomi un poco più avanti
sotto un cielo pesante, cupo
di nubi e poggia imminente,
presso la gloriosa devastata villa
di Marco Urrio Diomede:
sotto quell'ammasso di rovine
si apriva un giardinetto interno
con i resti di una fontana e un tempietto.
Due scale conducevano in un passaggio
sotterraneo circolare, pallidamente illuminato.
Anche qui era penetrata la mortale cenere...
Qui avevano trovato morte
diciotto tra donne e fanciulli, ora scheletri
cinerei che per trovare scampo
s'erano rifugiati in questa cantina
portando con sé acqua e cibo
ingannevole rifugio
presto divenuto la loro tomba.
Lì vicino, in altro luogo, parimenti soffocato
giaceva disteso al suolo il proprietario
della casa... Persa aveva la sua vita
a pochi passi dalla porta chiusa
la chiave ancora tra le dita.
Nei suoi pressi, accoccolato, un altro scheletro:
il suo fido servitore, nei pugni chiusi
monete d'oro e d'argento.

I find myself a short time afterward
under an oppressive sky, grown dark
with clouds and with impending rain,
near the glorious devastated villa
of Marcus Arrius Diomedes:
underneath the heap of ruins there
was the entrance to an interior garden
with the remains of a fountain and a shrine.
Two staircases led to an underground
circular passageway, palely illuminated.
The deadly ash had penetrated even to here...
Here they had found eighteen
women and children dead, now ashgray
skeletons who, seeking to escape,
carrying food and water with them,
had taken shelter in this underground
deceptive refuge
that had quickly turned into their tomb.
In another spot near them, also suffocated,
the owner of the house was lying stretched
at full length on the ground... He'd lost his life
just a few steps from the closed door,
the key still in his hand.
Nestled nearby, another skeleton:
his faithful servant, gold and silver coins
clutched in his fists.

Ma assai più forte
dell'imperante Morte
era già in me la nostalgia
di rivederla. E proprio
in un angolo del portico ove mi aggiravo
sconsolato la vidi all'improvviso
riapparire. Era proprio lei
seduta su un alto gradino
i suoi piedi penzoloni
nelle scarpe color sabbia.
Il mio primo moto fu di fuggir via
tra due colonne del giardino. Ma
mi fermò la sua voce... Mi parlava
mi interrogava con pacata ironia
insieme a un sorriso lieve e gaio
pian piano scioglieva l'intrico del mio
rovello. "Ti è riuscito poi
di acchiapparla quella mosca
sulla mia mano? Hai fatto tutta questa strada
per far di me esperienza
quando avresti potuto restare dov'eri...
a due passi della tua abitazione
c'è la mia finestra e la gabbia
con dentro un canarino... Bambini,
giocavamo insieme
e insieme ci *pattuffavamo*."

But even stronger
than overmastering Death
was the longing within me
to see her again. And indeed,
in a corner of the portico where I wandered
disconsolately, I saw her suddenly
reappear. She was really there,
seated on a high step
with her feet dangling
in sand-colored shoes.
My first impulse was to run away
between two of the garden's columns. But
I was stopped by her voice… She spoke to me,
she questioned me with placid irony
coupled with a bright vivacious smile,
bit by bit she undid the knot of my
vexation. "Did you manage after all
to get hold of that fly
that was on my hand? Have you come all this way
to have an experience of me
when you could have easily stayed where you were…
just a stone's throw away from where you live
is my window and a cage
with a canary… When we were little children
we used to play together
and sometimes we would tussle with each other."

Ah Gradiva, Zoe, Gradiva! Allora...
allora non più assurde
erano state le sue domande,
cancellata ogni mia follìa
se duemila anni prima avevo con lei
condiviso il pane, se solo a quel mitico
passato io ora sostituivo quello personale,
vero e magico d'infanzia, eco
della mia presente malinconia...

Ah, Gradiva, Zoe, Gradiva! Then...
then all her questions
no longer were absurd,
every bit of my madness was erased
if twenty centuries before I had
shared bread with her, if now I just replaced
that mythical past of ours with the personal,
actual, magical one of early childhood,
the echo of my present melancholy...

Dunque non greca o discendente
di Core, la viva e partecipe Zoe Bertgang
che mi parlava... Né greca né pompeiana
ma solo una compagna d'infanzia
a me assai vicina prima che divenissi
un insopportabile sofo, infermo
elucubratore, e perdipiù del tutto cieco
a ogni femminile grazia. "Aria pura
ero per te, divenuto arido e tedioso
come un cacatua impagliato
e insieme grandioso come un Archeotterige...
Ah, se solo tu volessi usare
a giusto fine la tua mente
(oggi assorbita dal sapere)
e la tua grandiosa fantasia!"
Così, la saggia e trasparente Zoe...
non di pietra o di bronzo costruita
ma vera e viva
agile e tranquilla, camminante e rilucente
dinanzi ai miei occhi
seppur negli anni da me rimossa e
non più riconosciuta.

Then neither Grecian nor descended from
Kore, the living, interacting Zoe Bertgang
who spoke to me... Neither Grecian nor Pompeiian
but merely a companion of my childhood
who had been very close to me before
I'd become an insufferable savant, an unhealthy
drudge, and, to top it off, completely blind
to every feminine grace. "I was pure air to you,
turned into something arid and tedious
as a stuffed cockatoo, and at the same time
as grandiose as an Archaeopteryx...
Ah, if only you had wished to put
your mind (that nowadays is all absorbed
in study and research) and your grandiose
imagination to some proper use!"
So spoke the wise and quite transparent Zoe...
not carved in stone or cast in bronze
but real and alive,
agile and tranquil, walking and radiant
before my eyes,
though taken from me by the years and now
no longer recognized.

V

Immagine rimossa... ma in
grado di ritornare per puro
amore di dottrina! Quella
che ci tiene lontani dalla vita...
Dunque fedele nell'infedeltà
perché dimenticare non vuol dire eliminare
ciò a cui si era legati. Rimozione
non è dissoluzione del ricordo.
Quanto è da noi rimosso non s'impone
sotto forma di ricordo, frutto
proibito o sublime sogno, ma resta
capace d'operare e di produrre effetti
sotto influssi di eventi
esterni, psichiche conseguenze
trasformazioni incomprensibili
se non in un erotico sentire.
La natura cacciata con la forca
continua a ritornare... né più né meno
come avvenne a quel pittore asceta
che al posto del Signore sulla croce
vide radiosa l'immagine
di una voluttuosa donna nuda...
daß das Verdrängte bei seiner Wiederkehr
aus dem Verdrängenden selbst hervortritt.

V

An image removed... but still
able to return through pure
love of scholarship! That
which keeps us far from life...
Faithful, then, in unfaithfulness
because forgetting doesn't mean erasing
what it was fastened to. To remove
is not to dissolve memory.
What's taken from us does not impose
itself in the form of memory, forbidden
fruit, or a sublime dream, but remains
able to work and generate its effects
under the influence of external
events, of psychic consequences,
incomprehensible transformations,
or else in an erotic sensation.
Nature driven off with a pitchfork
keeps coming back... neither more nor less
than was the case with that ascetic painter
who in place of the Lord upon the cross
beheld in all its radiance
the image of a voluptuous naked woman...
daß das Verdrängte bei seiner Wiederkehr
aus dem Verdrängenden selbst hervortritt.

*Che si debba dunque prima morire
per ritornare o divenire vivi? "Questa
forse la regola o fantasia, almeno
per chi ha eletto per amore di professione
la cara archeologia..."*

*So then what should we do before we die
to come back or to come alive?* "This might be
the rule or the fantasy, at least for those
who have chosen, out of love for the profession,
precious archaeology..."

Fu questo il nostro
ultimo appuntamento.
Aveva smesso di piovere,
ci avviammo, con il mio animo sgombro,
grazie alla serena Zoe-Gradiva,
mio dolce presente,
verso l'uscita di Pompei.
Trasformata come per incanto
era ora la Via dei Sepolcri
il cielo terso senza nubi risplendeva
nuovamente in alto,
un tappeto d'oro il suo lastricato
tutta l'antica città dissepolta,
invece di cenere e lapilli,
mi appariva coperta
di perle di diamanti… come gli occhi
della mia Zoe Bertgang Gradiva…

This was the last
of our meetings.
The rain had ceased to fall,
and so we set out, with my spirit freed,
thanks to the serene Zoe-Gradiva,
my sweet present,
toward the road that led out of Pompei.
The Street of Sepulchers was now transformed
as if a magic spell had been pronounced,
the clear and cloudless sky was freshly shining
above our heads,
the pavement turned into a golden carpet,
the entire ancient city, disinterred,
seemed to me to be covered
not with ashes and hardened lava
but pearls and diamonds… like the eyes
of my Zoe Bertgang Gradiva…

Giunti alla Porta d'Ercolano
là dove la strada consolare
ha per pavimento le antiche pietre laviche
mi fermai...
Pregai Zoe Gradiva rediviva di precedermi...
Sorridente, lei capì la mia estrema fantasia.
Sollevò un po' l'abito con la mano
e avvolta dal mio sguardo
trasognato, attraversò agile
e leggera quel lastricato
sotto un sole che tutto sfavillava
sogno, visione ed esistenza vera.

When we had come to the Gate of Hercules
there where the consular road
is paved with the ancient lava stones
I stopped...
I asked Zoe Gradiva rediviva to precede me...
Smiling, she understood my final fancy.
She raised her dress a little with one hand
and, enveloped in my dreamy
gaze, she crossed the road
with a light and lively step
under a sun that lit up everything —
dream, vision, and reality — with its glow.

Perfetta era nel suo incedere
la corrispondenza con la figura primigenia
dei miei ossessivi studi, la stessa
che tanto tempo prima io avevo visto
dalla mia finestra, la stessa che
precipitatomi per strada
non avevo raggiunta...
L'amore trionfava e
trovava appagamento quel mio delirio,
bello
prezioso
quanto passeggero
come prezioso
bello
ed effimero
del nostro esistere
è ogni vero incantamento
forza di vivere
attimo eterno.

Mount Sinai, Long Island, agosto–ottobre 2010

In her majestic stride I saw a perfect
correspondence with the primordial figure
of my obsessive studies, the same one
that I had seen so many years before
from my window, the same one
that I hadn't overtaken
as I rushed along the street...
Love had triumphed and
my delirium had found fulfillment,
beautiful
precious
so transient
as precious
beautiful
and ephemeral
is every true enchantment
of our existence,
the strength to live
an eternal moment.

Mount Sinai, Long Island, August–October 2010

NOTA DELL'AUTORE

Credo che questo racconto-in-versi o poema narrativo — secondo una lontana ma per me fertile suggestione a suo tempo indicata da Nelo Risi nel suo bellissimo libro *Di certe cose che dette in versi suonano meglio che in prosa* — debba essere accompagnato da alcune mie chiose e riflessioni.

Comincio dal titolo da me dato a questa "fantasia onirica". Il quale fa riferimento — ricalcandone la storia — sia a un singolare racconto di Wilhelm Jensen da lui pubblicato nel 1903 (Jensen gli aveva dato come sottotitolo *Fantasia pompeiana*), sia alla straordinaria lettura/riscrittura critica fattane da Sigmund Freud nel 1906 (*Gradiva. Delirio e sogni nella "Gradiva" di Wilhelm Jensen*), lettura per altro a lui suggerita da Carl Gustav Jung. Si tratta di due opere assiali che fin dai miei anni universitari mi hanno intensamente coinvolto sul piano emotivo e intellettivo.

Tra l'agosto e il settembre del 2010, per alcune ragioni di studio, mi è capitato di rileggerle, procurandomi un rinnovato piacere. L'edizione a cui mi riferisco è il volume complessivo *Gradiva*, curato da Cesare Musatti per Boringhieri (1961). Da questa rilettura più "matura" mi è sùbito nato l'impulso a scrivere un testo poetico che di queste opere ripercorresse emotivamente e riflessivamente l'indubbia (per me, anzi, accresciuta) fascinazione.

Considero, in ogni caso, questo mio poema narrativo un esperimento, non so quanto felice o riuscito. Sarà il lettore a deciderlo. Un esperimento anche o soprattutto linguistico (riprodurre in poesia, con un proprio ritmo, l'aura magica e *remota* nella quale si svolge la vicenda narrata da Jensen e così acutamente ripercorsa da Freud); un esperimento che, fra l'altro, ha avuto una sorprendente velocità d'esecuzione, proponendosi come una sorta di rovello o "brusìo" interiore che probabilmente mi portavo dentro da tempo. Mi sento in effetti "felice" di aver per così dire saldato un debito con me stesso.

Nel denominare questo testo "Poema" non c'è da parte mia nessuna pretenziosità, ma soltanto, appunto, la volontà di indicare la sua specifica natura metatestuale e, al contempo, il suo carattere di narrazione lirica, scandita in cinque Canti.

E ora alcune brevi chiose più dettagliate, forse non inutili per il lettore.

Il personaggio femminile di questo poema narrativo racchiude due figure in una sola: *Gradiva* (nome di un bassorilievo in stile neoattico conservato nei Musei Vaticani) e *Zoe Bertgang*. Due personaggi e due nomi che semanticamente si equivalgono. "Gradiva" si riallaccia al dio della guerra Marte, che gli antichi poeti greci chiamavano esattamente Marte Gradivo, ossia il *dio marciante verso il combattimento*. Nel racconto di Jensen l'archeologo Norbert Hanold dà questo nome all'immagine del bassorilievo, che lui sta appassionatamente studiando, raffigurante una giovane donna camminante. Pochi decenni dopo André Breton darà a Gradiva l'appellativo di *celle qui avançe*. Ma anche *Bertgang* (il cognome del personaggio femminile del racconto di Jensen), come ci ricorda Freud, ha un significato analogo, e cioè: *colei che risplende nel camminare*, in quanto *bert* ha in sé il significato di "rilucere", e *gang* di "andare". Il suo nome "Zoe" in greco significa "vita".

Secondo la mitologia antica ai morti veniva concesso di ritornare sulla terra per brevissimi periodi di tempo, a volte anche soltanto per poche ore o una manciata di minuti. Al momento dello scadere del loro tempo terreno una farfalla, messaggera dell'Ade, aveva il compito, svolazzando attorno allo spirito, di avvertirlo ch'era giunto il momento di rientrare nel regno dell'oltretomba.

Meleagro, eroe greco, figlio di Eneo (re di Calidone) e di Altea, è personaggio dell'*Iliade*. La sua vicenda è legata a una celebre caccia alla quale partecipò con una schiera di altri eroi per liberare il paese da un enorme cinghiale, inviato da Artemide sdegnata contro Eneo. Nel Museo Archeologico Nazionale di Napoli c'è un affresco che raffigura Meleagro insieme con la sua compagna Atalanta (descritta da Ovidio nelle *Metamorfosi*), ritrovato in una casa della Via di Mercurio nell'antica Pompei, affresco che aveva dato il nome alla casa stessa. Nel racconto di Jensen viene avanzata l'ipotesi che un discendente di un altro Meleagro, poeta greco vissuto qualche decennio prima della distruzione di Pompei, sarebbe vissuto a Pompei e avrebbe costruito la sua casa in Via di Mercurio.

L'asfodelo è pianta mediterranea delle Gigliacee, con lunghe foglie e fiori a pannocchia bianchi. Secondo l'antica tradizione greca il fiore era associato alle ombre dei trapassati, ed era in effetti usato per onorare i loro sepolcri.

La Casa del Fauno era una delle più lussuose abitazioni private dell'antica Pompei. Il nome della casa non deriva da quella del proprietario bensì dalla statuetta di bronzo (ora al Museo Archeologico Nazionale di Napoli) raffigurante un Fauno danzante, posto al centro dell'*impluvium* principale.

Archeotterige (o Archeopterige), quinta strofa, Canto IV: è il più antico rappresentante conosciuto della famiglia degli Uccelli. Il nome è composto dal greco *archáios* ("primitivo") e *ptérix* ("ala"). Visse nel tardo periodo giurassico, circa 150 milioni di anni fa, nell'Europa centrale (in particolare in quella che oggi sarebbe la Germania meridionale), quando questo continente era un arcipelago di varie isole dal clima tropicale. Era un volatile, un po' simile a un corvo gigantesco, munito di penne, mascelle con i denti, ali enormi terminanti in dita con unghie, coda lucertoliforme; qualcosa a metà strada tra i dinosauri e gli uccelli. Il primo completo specimen di Archeotterige fu annunciato nel 1861.

"Insieme ci *pattuffavamo*": la frase di Freud nella quale compare questo verbo così curioso, è tradotta da Cesare Musatti in questo modo: "Può darsi che, quando andavamo ogni giorno in giro insieme da buoni amici, e anche per cambiare ci bisticciavamo e ci pattuffavamo, io fossi diversa" (143). Il verbo in questione, in veneto (però scritto con una sola *t*), significa bisticciare o picchiare, ma non in modo violento, quasi in modo affettuoso. Anche nel dialetto triestino-friulano ("patufar", "patufarse") significa picchiarsi, schiaffeggiarsi, azzuffarsi, ed è voce che troviamo in Italo Svevo. Ringrazio amichevolmente i colleghi Dario Brancato, Giorgio Cadorini, Emanuele Cervato, Cristina Perissinotto e Nicoletta Pireddu per avermi variamente illuminato su questo verbo.

I versi in corsivo nella prima strofa dell'ultimo canto ("La natura cacciata con la forca continua a ritornare"), riportati da Freud e da me utilizzati anche in uno degli eserghi di questo libro, sono di Orazio (*Epistole*, I, 20, 24): *Natura furca espellas, semper redibit*. Il poeta latino dice propriamente: *Naturam expellas furca, tamen usque recurret* (Anche se cacci la natura con la forca, questa continuerà a ritornare).

L'artista-asceta ricordato da Freud, che al posto del Cristo sulla croce ritrasse l'immagine di una voluttuosa donna nuda, è Félicien Rops (1833-1898), pittore e incisore belga. La celebre quanto scandalosa opera a cui Freud fa riferimento è *La tentazione di sant'Antonio*, composta da Rops nel 1878, nella quale, appunto, al posto del Cristo crocifisso, appare il corpo di una donna nuda.

La citazione in tedesco tratta dalla *Gradiva* di Freud viene tradotta da Musatti in questo modo: "Egli [Rops] sembra aver saputo che quando il rimosso ritorna, sorge dallo stesso elemento rimosso".

Desidero ringraziare Paolo Lagazzi e Giancarlo Pontiggia attenti lettori del mio manoscritto. Ringrazio inoltre Donna

Sammis, direttrice dell'Interlibrary Loan della mia università, e il collega germanista Robert Bloomer per la loro collaborazione.

AUTHOR'S NOTE

I feel that this tale in verse or narrative poem—according to a distant but for me fertile suggestion given by Nelo Risi in his superb book *Regarding Certain Things That Sound Better When Said in Verse Than in Prose*—ought to be accompanied by a few glosses and reflections from me.

I begin with the title that I have given to this "oneiric fantasy." It refers—as I retrace its history—both to a singular tale by Wilhelm Jensen that he published in 1903 (Jensen gave it the subtitle *A Pompeiian Fantasia*) and to the extraordinary critical reading/rewriting of it done by Sigmund Freud in 1906 (*Gradiva: Delirium and Dreams in Wilhelm Jensen's "Gradiva"*), a reading, moreover, that was suggested to him by Carl Gustav Jung. These two axial works have intensely engaged me on both an emotional and an intellectual level since my undergraduate years.

Between August and September of 2010, I happened to reread both of them for certain scholarly purposes, providing a renewed pleasure for myself. The edition I used is the comprehensive volume *Gradiva*, edited and translated by Cesare Musatti for the publisher Boringhieri in 1961. From this more "mature" rereading there was quickly born in me an impulse to write a work of poetry that would emotionally and reflectively retrace the undeniable (in fact, enhanced) fascination that these texts have for me.

At any rate, I consider this narrative poem of mine to be an experiment. I don't know how happy or successful a one it is. That will be for the reader to decide. An experiment that is also or principally linguistic (to reproduce in poetry, with an appropriate rhythm, the magical and *distant* aura in which the event unfolds that is narrated by Jensen and so acutely retraced by Freud); an experiment that, among other things, has had a surprising swiftness of execution, presenting itself as a kind of disturbance or interior "buzz" that I had probably carried inside myself for some time. In fact I feel "happy" to have, so to speak, settled a debt with myself.

In calling this text a "Poema" [*note*: a more extended and often more exalted text than a *poesia*, i.e., a lyric] there is no pretension on my part, but only, in truth, the desire to indicate its specific metatextual nature and, at the same time, its character as a lyrical narrative, articulated in five cantos.

And now a few brief but more detailed glosses, which may be of some use to the reader.

The female character in this narrative poem combines two figures in one: *Gradiva* (the name of a bas-relief in the neo-Attic style held in the Vatican Museums) and *Zoe Bertgang*. Two characters and two names that are semantically equivalent. "Gradiva" refers to the war god Mars, whom the ancient Greek poets specifically called Mars Gradivus: that is, the *god marching toward combat*. In Jensen's tale the archaeologist Norbert Hanold gives this name to the image on the bas-relief, representing a walking young woman, which he is passionately studying. A few decades later André Breton will designate Gradiva *celle qui avançe*. But *Bertgang* (the last name of the female character in Jensen's narrative), as Freud reminds us, also has an analogous meaning, namely: *she who shines while walking*, in which *bert* has the sense of "glittering," and *gang* that of "moving." Her name, Zoe, means "life" in Greek.

According to ancient mythology, it happened that the dead were permitted to return to earth for very brief periods of time, in some instances for only a few hours or even just a handful of minutes. At the moment when their time on earth expired, a butterfly, the messenger of Hades, fluttering around the spirit, had the task of advising it that the time had arrived for it to re-enter the realm of the underworld.

Meleager, a Greek hero, son of Oeneus (king of Calydon) and Althaea, is a character in the *Iliad*. His adventure is connected to a celebrated hunt in which he took part with a group of other heroes to rid the countryside of a huge wild boar, which had been dispatched against Oeneus by the scorned Artemis. In the National Archaeological Museum of Naples there is a fresco that depicts Meleager together with his companion Atalanta (who is described by Ovid in the *Metamorphoses*), rediscovered in a house on the Street of Mercury in ancient Pompeii, a fresco that had given its name to that house. In his tale Jensen puts forward the supposition that a descendant of another Meleager, a Greek poet who lived several decades before the destruction of Pompeii, had lived in Pompeii and had built the house in question.

The asphodel is a liliaceous Mediterranean plant, with long leaves and white clustered flowers. According to ancient Greek tradition, the flower was associated with the shades of the deceased and was in fact used to adorn their tombs.

The House of the Faun was one of the most luxurious private residences of ancient Pompeii. The name of the house derives not from that of its owner but instead from a bronze statuette (now in the National Archaeological Museum of Naples) depicting a dancing Faun, placed in the middle of the main *impluvium*.

Archeopterix (fifth stanza of Canto IV) is the oldest known representative of the bird family. Its name is formed from the Greek *archáios* ("primitive") e *ptérix* ("wing"). It lived in the late Jurassic period, around 150,000 years ago, in central Europe (especially in what would today be southern Germany), when that continent was an archipelago of various islands with a tropical climate. It was a winged creature, a bit like a giant raven, furnished with feathers, jaws containing teeth, enormous wings ending in digits with nails, and a lizardlike tail; something halfway between a dinosaur and a bird. The discovery of the first complete specimen of an Archeopterix was announced in 1861.

"Sometimes we would *tussle* with each other": the sentence of Freud's in which this very odd word appears is translated by Cesare Musatti as follows: "Può darsi che, quando andavamo ogni giorno in giro insieme da buoni amici, e anche per cambiare ci bisticciavamo e ci pattuffavamo, io fossi diversa" ("It may be that, when we went around together every day as good friends, and even wrangled and cuffed each other for a change, I was different" (143). The verb in question, in the Veneto dialect (but spelled with only one *t*), means "to wrangle or strike," but in an almost affectionate way, not a violent one. Likewise in the Triestine-Friulano dialect (*patufar, patufarse*) it signifies "striking, slapping, scuffling," and is a term found in Italo Svevo. My most cordial thanks to my colleagues Dario Brancato, Giorgio Cadorini, Emanuele Cervato, Cristina Perissinotto, and Nicoletta Pireddu for having variously illuminated this verb for me.

The lines in italics in the first stanza of the last canto ("Nature driven off with a pitchfork keeps coming back"), quoted by Freud and also used by me as one of the epigraphs of this book, are from Horace (*Epistles*, I, 10, 24): *Natura furca espellas, semper redibit.* The Latin poet actually writes: *Naturam expellas furca, tamen usque recurret* (Even if you drive nature off with a pitchfork, it will keep coming back).

The artist-ascetic recalled by Freud, who in place of Christ on the cross depicted the image of a voluptuous nude woman, is the Belgian painter and engraver Félicien Rops (1833-1898). The celebrated though shocking work to which Freud refers is *The Temptation of Saint Anthony*, done by

Rops in 1878, in which, indeed, in place of the crucified Christ appears the body of a naked woman.

The German quotation taken from Freud's *Gradiva* is translated by Musatti as follows: "Egli [Rops] sembra aver saputo che quando il rimosso ritorna, sorge dallo stesso elemento rimosso" ("He [Rops] seems to have known that when what was repressed returns, it emerges from that very same repressed element").

I wish to thank Paolo Lagazzi and Giancarlo Pontiggia, attentive readers of my manuscript. I also thank Donna Sammis, interlibrary loan director at my university, and Robert Bloomer, my colleague in the German Department, for their assistance.

ABOUT THE AUTHOR AND TRANSLATOR

LUIGI FONTANELLA lives in Florence, Rome, and New York. Professor Emeritus of Italian Languages and Literature at the State University of New York (Stony Brook), he is a poet, critic, novelist, and dramatist. The recipient of many literary awards, he has published more than forty volumes of poetry, fiction, and essays, among the most recent of which are *L'adolescenza e la notte* (2015; translated by Giorgio Mobili as *Adolescence and Night*, 2021); *Il dio di New York* (2017; translated by Siân E. Gibby as *The God of New York*, Bordighera Press, 2022); *Lo scialle rosso: Poemetti e racconti in versi* (2017); *Monte Stella: Poesie 2014-2019* (2020); *Raccontare la poesia (1970-2020): Saggi, ricordi, testimonianze critiche* (2021); *Tre passi nel desiderio: Tre atti unici* (2021); and *Dell'ultimo orizzonte: Poesie scelte 1970-2021* (2023). He is the founder and director of IPA (Italian Poetry in America), and senior editor of the journal *Gradiva* and chief editor of its associated series of bilingual volumes.

MICHAEL PALMA's poetry collections are *The Egg Shape* (1972), *Antibodies* (1997), *A Fortune in Gold* (2000), *Begin in Gladness* (2011), and *Local Colors* (2025), as well as an internet chapbook, *The Ghost of Congress Street: Selected Poems*. He is also the author of *Faithful in My Fashion: Essays on the Translation of Poetry* (2016). His twenty translations of modern Italian poets include Luigi Fontanella's *The Transparent Life and Other Poems* (2000) and prize-winning volumes of Guido Gozzano and Diego Valeri with Princeton University Press. His fully rhymed translation of Dante's *Inferno* was published by Norton in 2002, and his translation of the complete *Commedia* was published by Liveright in December 2024.

Diaspora

As "diaspora" is the dispersion or spread of people from their original homeland, this book series takes its name in the intellectual spirit of willful dispersion of subject matter and thought. It is dedicated to publishing those studies and creative works that in various and sundry ways speak to or offer new methods of analysis and/or articulations of the Italian diaspora.

Carmelo Fucarino. *Two Italian Geniuses in New York: Broken American Dreams.* ISBN 978-1-955995-05-4. 2023

Anthony Julian Tamburri, ed. *Re-Thinking* The Godfather *50 Years Later.* ISBN 978-1-955995-06-1. 2024

Anthony Socci. *United We Stand. Pre WW II-Chronicles of the Italian Colony of Stamford.* ISBN 978-1-955995-07-8. 2024

Antonio D'Alfonso. *I Could Have Been a Contender. (On Five Films).* ISBN 978-1-955995-09-2. 2024

Antonio Vitti and Anthony Julian Tamburri, eds. *Studi mediterranei: bellezze e misteri. Mediterranean Studies: Beauty and Mystery.* ISBN 978-1-955995-10-8. 2024

Casa Lago Press Editorial Group

David Aliano
William Boelhower
Leonardo Buonomo
Ryan Calabretta-Sajder
Nancy Carnevale
Stephen J. Cerulli
Donna Chirico
Fred Gardaphé
Paolo A. Giordano
Nicolas Grosso

Donatella Izzo
John Kirby
Chiara Mazzucchelli
Emanuele Pettener
Mark Pietralunga
Joseph Sciorra
Ilaria Serra
Anthony Julian Tamburri
Sabrina Vellucci
Leslie Wilson

www.ingramcontent.com/pod-product-compliance
Lightning Source LLC
Chambersburg PA
CBHW051701040426
42446CB00009B/1249